Block Scheduling Implementation Guide

for

World History:
The Human Experience

GLENCOE
McGraw-Hill

New York, New York   Columbus, Ohio   Woodland Hills, California   Peoria, Illinois

CONTENTS

Benefits of Block Scheduling 1

Team Teaching 4

90-Minute Block Schedule Planning Guide 6

Implementing Block Scheduling in Your Classroom 10

Further Professional Reading 13

Block Scheduling opportunities are offered throughout the Teacher's Wrap-around Edition for this program. You will see the Glencoe Block Scheduling indicator following each teaching activity that would be appropriate for a block of class time. Use this handy guide to help you streamline your Block Scheduling lesson planning.

Copyright © by The McGraw-Hill Companies, Inc. All rights reserved. Permission is granted to reproduce the material contained herein on the condition that such material be reproduced only for classroom use; be provided to students, teachers, and families without charge; and be used solely in conjunction with *World History: The Human Experience.* Any other reproduction, for use or sale, is prohibited without prior written permission of the publisher.

Send all inquiries to:
Glencoe/McGraw-Hill
936 Eastwind Drive
Westerville, Ohio 43081

ISBN 0-02-823232-1

Printed in the United States of America

6 7 8 9 10 11 12   045   04 03 02 01 00 99

BENEFITS OF WORKING "ON THE BLOCK"

Class scheduling is an expression of the relationship between learning and time. Traditionally, schools schedule six or seven 40- to 55-minute classes per day. These classes usually meet for 180 school days per school year.

Block scheduling–or working "on the block" as many teachers call it–differs from traditional scheduling in that fewer class sessions are scheduled for larger blocks of time over fewer days. For example, in block scheduling, a course might meet for 90 minutes a day for 90 days, or half a school year. Does this type of scheduling have any advantage over more traditional scheduling methods? Those schools that have tried it believe it does.

■ ADVANTAGES FOR SCHOOL SYSTEMS

For the schools themselves, the greatest advantage of block scheduling is a better use of resources. The schedule change does not require additional teachers or classrooms. It eliminates half of the time needed for class changes, which results in fewer discipline problems. If two six-minute class changes are eliminated each day, an hour of teaching time is gained in just one week. Results from several high schools indicate significantly fewer suspensions and student dropouts due to improved student-teacher relationships. Schools also report an increase in the overall quality of teacher instruction and student time on task.

■ ADVANTAGES FOR TEACHERS

The advantages for teachers in schools that use block scheduling are many. These advantages fall into several categories.

Improved Teacher–Student Relationships

Teacher–student relationships are improved. In traditional scheduling, teachers may teach five or six (or more) classes a day with as many different preparations. They are expected to know and teach 150 or more students each day. With block scheduling, teachers have responsibility for a smaller number of students at a time, so students and teachers get to know each other better. With longer class periods, teachers can provide additional time and other resources for meeting the individual needs of students.

Focused Instruction

Teachers can also be more focused on what they are teaching. With more intensive teaching of a subject, it might be expected that teachers are more likely to "burn out" in block scheduling. However, the more manageable number of students per day and fewer preparations keep this from happening. Block scheduling seems to result in changes in teaching approaches, classrooms that are more student centered, improved teacher morale, and increased teacher effectiveness. Teachers feel free to venture away from discussion and lecture to use more productive models of teaching.

Time Efficiencies

If school days are of the same length as those that are more traditionally scheduled, teachers find the block approach more time efficient. Block scheduling cuts in half the time needed for introducing and closing classes. Block scheduling also eliminates half of the time needed for class changes. If two six-minute class changes are eliminated each day, an hour of teaching time is gained in just one week. Fewer class changes also result in fewer discipline problems.

Increased Flexibility

Flexibility is increased because less complex teaching schedules create more opportunities for cooperative teaching strategies, such as team teaching and interdisciplinary studies. Block scheduling also increases the number of nontraditional activity-based courses that can be offered.

■ ADVANTAGES FOR STUDENTS

The benefits of block scheduling are not limited to teachers. Students also benefit.

Long-Term Learning

The block scheduling format, due to its emphasis on in-depth study, appears to provide an environment that better accommodates how students learn and retain information. New research on how the brain functions shows that the brain—through its continual associations of ideas—relates incoming information to what is already known. Whereas traditional class settings use class time to dispense facts and drill, with students resorting to memorization for the short term, block sessions help students make deeper connections within their knowledge bases for the long term. In the schedule's blocks of uninterrupted focus, students more readily detect patterns—and thus meaning—between the whole of a concept and its parts. In addition, during a block students study fewer subjects each term, making their workload easier to manage. Students experience fewer outside distractions and are better able to concentrate.

Heightened Success Rates

Research indicates that block scheduling results in heightened student success rates because students seem to learn more and retain it better. Problem-solving skills are better developed, grades improve, and the failure rate drops.

Improved Relationships and Work

Some of the advantages for teachers also are advantages for students. Improved student-teacher relationships and more manageable workloads help students. Students feel better about what they are learning, outside interference is reduced, and students are better able to concentrate. Generally, students feel better organized and are more aware of their progress in the class.

Home-related Benefits

Parents report home-related benefits to block scheduling. There are fewer hassles about school, and students have a more positive attitude in general and take more responsibility for their homework. All of this results in a more relaxed family environment.

Curricular Advantages

Many curricular advantages are also present for students. At-risk students can be scheduled for required courses during the first term. If they do not pass the course, they can repeat it during the second term instead of taking an elective. This opportunity reduces the need for summer school or other remedial work. Better students can move ahead more quickly, and those students who develop a late interest in certain courses can take more of them. For example, a student can take two consecutive math courses in one year. Block scheduling has been shown to increase the number of students who take upper-level classes and earn advanced studies diplomas.

■ MODIFIED BLOCK SCHEDULING

Some schools use a modified form of block scheduling that combines two core classes. Under this system, students might study social studies for 90 minutes each day during the first semester and science during the second semester. Another modification has students taking English and social studies blocks in one semester and science and mathematics blocks in the second. Such scheduling encourages the teachers to institute team teaching or similar interdisciplinary approaches.

Questions About Block Scheduling Answered

The unique educational opportunity of Block Scheduling is being uncovered by teachers across the educational spectrum. Some surprising answers to questions have been revealed in this process.

Will all lessons have to be replanned to accommodate the extended class periods?

Overall, teachers have happily found that they can now cover all of the material they want to present with time to pursue topics in-depth and with a greater opportunity to fully address student needs. As class sessions are driven by content and skills assessment, they are also guided by a partnership between students and teachers to achieve the decided upon learning goals.

Will my understanding of students' abilities be increased and addressed through extended time together?

The majority of teachers report a much greater return of student understanding from the teachers' investment of time than they expected. Extended classes also allow for more easily addressing the needs of the different learning styles of students.

Will lower level students find the Block Scheduling format too challenging to their levels of concentration?

Reports indicate students feel less threatened by the extended class format which allows them more time to question the teachers about subject matter they don't understand. Block Scheduling also provides time for peer teaching and collaboration.

Will Block Scheduling be more work than it is worth to students and teachers?

Those teachers who have ventured into the Block Scheduling approach report that not only does it expand student learning, it also enriches and enlivens their own instruction.

TEAM TEACHING

■ BLOCK SCHEDULING AND TEAM TEACHING

Block Scheduling and Team Teaching often go hand in hand. While some schools have an integrated team structure with most teachers in teams, other schools may only encourage occasional team teaching.

Teachers of core subjects—English, mathematics, science, and social studies—often coordinate the block schedule in cooperation with one another so they can further concentrate unit study or conduct a special project.

Other teams may integrate the curriculum and merge the study and practice of language skills—reading, writing, grammar, listening, and speaking—with specific content study, weaving at least two disciplines within the block schedule. For example, the English teacher may teach students how to write business letters as a culminating activity for the science teacher's unit on environmental studies or the social studies teacher's lesson on United States lobbying practices. This integration formulates a unified approach to learning that, within a block schedule, is also time efficient.

■ GOALS OF TEAM TEACHING

The primary goal of collaboration—specifically Team Teaching—is to create a community of learners among all players—administrators, faculty, staff, students, and parents. This community sets clear goals, works together to reach them, and shares the responsibility for successes or failures.

Teachers who collaborate with one another interact ultimately to help students learn. Their interactions may involve trading resources, planning activities, sharing the results of a lesson, writing a mutual lesson plan, teaching a class together, analyzing how a failing student can achieve, or meeting with a student's parents.

When instructors share teaching practices, teach a class or course together, or help each other by observing and evaluating one another's teaching, they truly form a team—one that achieves collegiality, or shared authority among colleagues, which is consistently found in successful schools.

■ BENEFITS OF TEAM TEACHING

Researchers who have observed and interviewed teachers who teach in teams report significantly positive benefits. Team teachers perceive themselves as more empowered in a team than as an individual within a department structure. No longer are they isolated in their classrooms. Because members of teams regularly make plans together, they gain greater decision-making abilities and solve problems with more frequent success.

Teachers also report the team experience enhances their professional competence, and increases confidence in their abilities. Sharing team teaching experiences with other instructors at local, regional, and state conferences further expands their knowledge and proficiency.

TEACHING IN A TEAM

Teaching in a team requires hard work and frequent communication. Team teachers find that, with regular communication, they are able to discuss and resolve student learning and behavior problems quickly before they reach a crisis stage.

Team teachers also find they are better able to address students' different learning styles. In addition, the wealth of content material presented and students' skills refinement achieved further supports and edifies the team teaching experience.

Team members must commit themselves to collaboration to make the team a success. But the individual instructor need not sacrifice his or her uniqueness. Obviously, each teacher in the team has a distinctive teaching style, so the team functions best when its instructional plans capitalize on the strengths of each style.

Teaching teams whose members generally hold similar personal values and professional philosophies are the most successful. When this is not the case, fragmentation can be avoided if: (1) teachers choose or agree on their own partners, (2) the team creates a system for resolving conflict among its members, and (3) the team divides its responsibilities equitably.

TEAM TEACHING MAXIMS

Team Teaching Takes an Extraordinary Amount of Communication. Make time to meet regularly with team members away from other work or demands.

Clear and Enforced Rules Are a Necessity. Make sure students know from the start what rules for classroom behavior, attendance, tardiness, homework, and breaks are to be enforced. After teachers and students agree on the rules, enforce them consistently.

Teachers Learn to Create a Student-Centered Classroom. Be flexible; keep your class student-centered, task-oriented, and collaborative through open communication and a student partnership of shared ideas.

Team Teaching Can Be Fun. Choose activities for team teaching that create excitement for you, your partner, and your students. Don't be afraid to experiment with the great ideas you have that were previously shelved because of lack of time for development.

Other curriculum areas with which history teachers have had successful team teaching experiences include: Literature, Speech, English Composition, Mathematics, Science, Art, Music, and Tech. Prep., in addition to other social studies curricula.
Adapted from Raker 1994

90-MINUTE BLOCK SCHEDULE PLANNING GUIDE

The next few pages contain a block planning guide to use with *World History: The Human Experience*. It is a tool that you may adapt to your particular classroom needs and style of teaching.

To the right of each unit title in the guide is the suggested total number of days needed for that unit. This number is the sum of the days suggested to teach each chapter in that unit.

Although block scheduling need not be done in 90-minute units, that unit is the most common, and this guide is based on a total of 90 days of 90-minute periods. It may be easily adjusted for alternative lengths of time or for varied course emphasis.

UNIT/CHAPTER/SECTION	DAYS
Unit 1: The Rise of Civilizations	
Chapter 1: Human Beginnings	2
Section 1: Discovery of Early Humans in Africa	1/2
Section 2: The Appearance of *Homo Sapiens*	1/2
Section 3: Emergence of Civilization	1/2
Chapter Test and Review	1/2
Chapter 2: Early Civilizations	2 1/2
Section 1: The Nile Valley	1/2
Section 2: The Fertile Crescent	1/2
Section 3: Early South Asia	1/2
Section 4: Early China	1/2
Chapter Test and Review	1/2
Chapter 3: Kingdoms and Empires in the Middle East	2
Section 1: Trading Peoples	1/2
Section 2: Early Israelites	1/2
Section 3: Empire Builders	1/2
Chapter Test and Review	1/2
Unit 2: Flowering of Civilizations	
Chapter 4: The Rise of Ancient Greece	2 1/2
Section 1: Beginnings	1/2
Section 2: The Polis	1/2
Section 3: Rivals	1/2
Section 4: War, Glory, and Decline	1/2
Chapter Test and Review	1/2
Chapter 5: The Height of Greek Civilization	2
Section 1: Quest for Beauty and Meaning	1/2
Section 2: The Greek Mind	1/2
Section 3: Alexander's Empire	1/2
Chapter Test and Review	1/2
Chapter 6: Ancient Rome and Early Christianity	3
Section 1: The Roman Republic	1/2
Section 2: Expansion and Crisis	1/2
Section 3: The Roman Empire	1/2
Section 4: The Rise of Christianity	1/2
Section 5: Roman Decline	1/2
Chapter Test and Review	1/2
Chapter 7: Flowering of African Civilizations	2
Section 1: Early Africa	1/2
Section 2: Kingdoms of West Africa	1/2
Section 3: African Trading Cities and States	1/2
Chapter Test and Review	1/2

UNIT/CHAPTER/SECTION	DAYS
Chapter 8: India's Great Civilization	**2**
Section 1: Origins of Hindu India	1/2
Section 2: Rise of Buddhism	1/2
Section 3: Indian Empires	1/2
Chapter Test and Review	1/2
Chapter 9: China's Flourishing Civilization	**2**
Section 1: Three Great Dynasties	1/2
Section 2: Three Ways of Life	1/2
Section 3: Society and Culture	1/2
Chapter Test and Review	1/2

Unit 3: Regional Civilizations

Chapter 10: Byzantines and Slavs	**2**
Section 1: The New Rome	1/2
Section 2: Byzantine Civilization	1/2
Section 3: The Eastern Slaves	1/2
Chapter Test and Review	1/2
Chapter 11: Islamic Civilization	**2**
Section 1: A New Faith	1/2
Section 2: Spread of Islam	1/2
Section 3: Daily Life and Culture	1/2
Chapter Test and Review	1/2
Chapter 12: The Rise of Medieval Europe	**2 1/2**
Section 1: Frankish Rulers	1/2
Section 2: Medieval Life	1/2
Section 3: The Medieval Church	1/2
Section 4: Rise of European Monarchy	1/2
Chapter Test and Review	1/2
Chapter 13: Medieval Europe at Its Height	**2 1/2**
Section 1: The Crusades	1/2
Section 2: Economic and Cultural Revival	1/2
Section 3: Strengthening the Monarchy	1/2

UNIT/CHAPTER/SECTION	DAYS
Section 4: The Troubled Church	1/2
Chapter Test and Review	1/2
Chapter 14: East and South Asia	**2 1/2**
Section 1: Central Asia	1/2
Section 2: China	1/2
Section 3: Southeast Asia	1/2
Section 4: Korea and Japan	1/2
Chapter Test and Review	1/2
Chapter 15: The Americas	**2**
Section 1: The Early Americas	1/2
Section 2: Early Mesoamerican Cultures	1/2
Section 3: The Aztec and Inca Empires	1/2
Chapter Test and Review	1/2

Unit 4: Emergence of the Modern World

Chapter 16: Renaissance and Reformation	**3**
Section 1: The Italian Renaissance	1/2
Section 2: The Northern Renaissance	1/2
Section 3: The Protestant Reformation	1/2
Section 4: The Spread of Protestantism	1/2
Section 5: The Catholic Reformation	1/2
Chapter Test and Review	1/2
Chapter 17: Expanding Horizons	**2**
Section 1: Early Explorations	1/2
Section 2: Overseas Empires	1/2
Section 3: Changing Ways of Life	1/2
Chapter Test and Review	1/2
Chapter 18: Empires of Asia	**2 1/2**
Section 1: Muslim Empires	1/2
Section 2: Chinese Dynasties	1/2
Section 3: The Japanese Empire	1/2

UNIT/CHAPTER/SECTION	DAYS
Section 4: Southeast Asia	1/2
Chapter Test and Review	1/2
Chapter 19: Royal Power and Conflict	**2 1/2**
Section 1: Spain	1/2
Section 2: England	1/2
Section 3: France	1/2
Section 4: The German States	1/4
Section 5: Russia	1/4
Chapter Test and Review	1/2

Unit 5: Age of Revolution

Chapter 20: Scientific Revolution	**2**
Section 1: New Scientific Ideas	1/2
Section 2: Impact of Science	1/2
Section 3: Triumph of Reason	1/2
Chapter Test and Review	1/2
Chapter 21: English and American Revolutions	**2 1/2**
Section 1: Civil War	1/2
Section 2: A King Returns to the Throne	1/2
Section 3: Road to Revolt	1/2
Section 4: A War for Independence	1/2
Chapter Test and Review	1/2
Chapter 22: The French Revolution	**3**
Section 1: The Old Order	1/2
Section 2: Constitutional Government	1/2
Section 3: Dawn of a New Era	1/2
Section 4: Napoleon's Empire	1/2
Section 5: Peace in Europe	1/2
Chapter Test and Review	1/2

Unit 6: Industry and Nationalism

Chapter 23: Age of Industry	**2 1/2**
Section 1: Living from the Land	1/2

UNIT/CHAPTER/SECTION	DAYS
Section 2: The Beginnings of Change	1/2
Section 3: The Growth of Industry	1/2
Section 4: A New Society	1/2
Chapter Test and Review	1/2
Chapter 24: Cultural Revolution	**2 1/2**
Section 1: New Ideas	1/2
Section 2: The New Science	1/2
Section 3: Popular Culture	1/2
Section 4: Revolution in the Arts	1/2
Chapter Test and Review	1/2
Chapter 25: Democracy and Reform	**3**
Section 1: Reform in Great Britain	1/2
Section 2: The Dominions	1/2
Section 3: Political Struggles in France	1/2
Section 4: Expansion of the United States	1/2
Section 5: Latin American Independence	1/2
Chapter Test and Review	1/2
Chapter 26: Reaction and Nationalism	**3**
Section 1: The Unification of Italy	1/2
Section 2: The Unification of Germany	1/2
Section 3: Bismarck's Realm	1/2
Section 4: Empires of the Czars	1/2
Section 5: Austria–Hungary's Decline	1/2
Chapter Test and Review	1/2
Chapter 27: The Age of Imperialism	**2 1/2**
Section 1: Pressures for Expansion	1/2
Section 2: The Partition of Africa	1/2
Section 3: The Division of Asia	1/2
Section 4: Imperialism in the Americas	1/2
Chapter Test and Review	1/2

UNIT/CHAPTER/SECTION	DAYS
Unit 7: World in Conflict	
Chapter 28: World War I	**3**
Section 1: The Seeds of War	1/2
Section 2: The Spark	1/2
Section 3: The War	1/2
Section 4: The Russian Revolution	1/2
Section 5: Peace at Last	1/2
Chapter Test and Review	1/2
Chapter 29: Between Two Fires	**2 1/2**
Section 1: The Postwar World	1/2
Section 2: The Western Democracies	1/2
Section 3: Fascist Dictatorships	1/2
Section 4: The Soviet Union	1/2
Chapter Test and Review	1/2
Chapter 30: Nationalism in Asia, Africa, and Latin America	**3**
Section 1: New Forces in the Middle East and Africa	1/2
Section 2: India's Struggle for Independence	1/2
Section 3: China's Drive for Modernization	1/2
Section 4: Militarism in Japan	1/2
Section 5: Nationalism in Latin America	1/2
Chapter Test and Review	1/2
Chapter 31: World War II	**3**
Section 1: The Path to War	1/2
Section 2: War in Europe	1/2
Section 3: A Global Conflict	1/2
Section 4: Turning Points	1/2
Section 5: Allied Victories	1/2
Chapter Test and Review	1/2
Unit 8: The Contemporary World	
Chapter 32: The Cold War	**2 1/2**
Section 1: The East–West Split	1/2
Section 2: The Communist Bloc	1/2
Section 3: Western Europe	1/2

UNIT/CHAPTER/SECTION	DAYS
Section 4: The United States and Canada	1/2
Chapter Test and Review	1/2
Chapter 33: Asia and the Pacific	**3**
Section 1: Japan's Economic Rise	1/2
Section 2: China and the Revolution	1/2
Section 3: A Divided Korea	1/2
Section 4: Southeast Asia	1/2
Section 5: South Asia	1/4
Section 6: The Pacific	1/4
Chapter Test and Review	1/2
Chapter 34: Africa	**2**
Section 1: African Independence	1/2
Section 2: Africa Today	1/2
Section 3: Africa's Challenges	1/2
Chapter Test and Review	1/2
Chapter 35: The Middle East	**2**
Section 1: Nationalism in the Middle East	1/2
Section 2: War and Peace in the Middle East	1/2
Section 3: Challenges Facing the Middle East	1/2
Chapter Test and Review	1/2
Chapter 36: Latin America	**2 1/2**
Section 1: Latin American Challenges	1/2
Section 2: Mexico and the Caribbean	1/2
Section 3: Central America	1/2
Section 4: South America	1/2
Chapter Test and Review	1/2
Chapter 37: The World in Transition	**2 1/2**
Section 1: The End of the Cold War	1/4
Section 2: The Crumbling Wall	1/2
Section 3: Toward a European Union	1/2
Section 4: National and Ethnic Conflicts	1/2
Section 5: Global Interdependence	1/4
Chapter Test and Review	1/2

IMPLEMENTING BLOCK SCHEDULING IN YOUR CLASSROOM

World History: The Human Experience includes components that will facilitate your use of block scheduling and make possible a more in-depth study of important social studies concepts. A wealth of blackline masters allows students to work individually to reinforce their understanding of previously taught material. Because students are in the classroom for extended periods, they may use many of these materials during class sessions. Teachers can then immediately identify students who are having difficulty with major concepts and plan remediation activities—either individually or in peer groups.

Blackline masters suited for such uses include:
- *Guided Reading Activities*
- *Reteaching Activities*
- *Enrichment Activities*
- *People in World History*
- *Historical Significance Chapter Activities*

World History: The Human Experience provides unique opportunities for individual and group projects, multimedia applications, and extension.

■ INDIVIDUAL AND GROUP PROJECTS

The expanded class periods inherent in block scheduling help ensure that students will receive feedback on their progress more quickly than in traditional classrooms. Teachers can assess which students might need extra help with certain concepts along with those students who might need additional challenges.

Testmaker

Testmaker software enables you to create assessment tools in a way that reflects your course of study, allowing for more precise and accurate assessment and more appropriate feedback. Because block scheduling involves longer class periods, you may use the *Testmaker* to construct more comprehensive tests.

Transparencies

World History: The Human Experience also includes a variety of transparencies that help teachers introduce key concepts. The *Teaching Transparencies* incorporate teaching notes to expand on all units of study in the text. *Mapping History Transparencies* incorporate geographic concepts into your course of study, providing for a more complete picture of the world. *Chapter Transparencies* use computer generated graphics to present important concepts in an interesting and unique way. Teaching transparencies and student activities aid in student understanding. *World History and Art Transparencies* enable you to link the arts with your classroom experience.

■ MULTIMEDIA APPLICATIONS

Today's students have grown up with computers and televisions. As a result, they are often most receptive to multimedia stimuli. The *World History: The Human Experience* program provides such stimuli in several formats.

Videotapes, Videodiscs, and CD-Roms

The students' learning experience is often enhanced by videotapes and videodiscs that bring concepts to them in a format they enjoy. In association with National Geographic Society, Glencoe offers many materials that highlight issues of interest in today's world in ways that stimulate enthusiasm for learning. The uninterrupted periods of block scheduling allow you to present these materials and follow them up with discussion during the same period. The following materials are available:
- *STV: Maya*
- *STV: World Geography*
- *STV: North America*
- *NGS Picture Show™*
  Ancient Civilizations: Egypt and the Fertile Crescent
  Ancient Civilizations: India and China
  Ancient Civilizations: The Americas
  The Middle Ages
  The Renaissance
  Great Explorers, Parts 1 and 2
  Picture Atlas of the World
- *GTV: A Geographic Perspective on American History*
- *GTV: The American People: Fabric of a Nation*

From ABCNews Interactive™, the following videodiscs help students in their understanding of world history with a dramatic presentation of leaders, events, and issues of the past and present.
- *Lessons of War*
- *Communism and the Cold War*
- *In the Holy Land*
- *Turning Points in World History*

These audio and visual selections are ideal for block scheduling. Because of the extended class periods, you have enough time to introduce a lesson with a transparency, discuss the lesson, and play a video segment for enrichment.

■ EXTENSION AND ENRICHMENT

World History: The Human Experience provides you and your students with ample opportunities to enrich and extend the textbook content.

Materials Available

The following components not only reinforce the topics and skills introduced in your class sessions, but incorporate elements from other disciplines, as well, promoting a complete and well-rounded course of study.
- *Skill Reinforcement Activities*
- *Source Readings*
- *World Literature Selections*
- *Writer's Guidebook*
- *Outline Map Resource Book*
- *Focus on World Art Prints*

Each of these components can be used alone or in a supplemental fashion, allowing for flexibility of implementation. They may be introduced in a classroom setting and utilized either as independent study material or on a class-wide basis.

Uses in Block Scheduling

Because of their flexibility, these ancillary materials are particularly suited to block scheduling. Students may study the textbook lesson during the first portion of the class period. They may then go on to work with the extension and enrichment activities or supplementary readings to build on their understanding of the text material. Because the students are in the classroom for longer periods, the teacher can monitor student understanding of basic concepts as the class works through the various components of the program. In this way, teachers can spot students who might need to review basic concepts as well as those who might need more challenges. The teacher can then provide these reviews and challenges immediately.

The use of multimedia in block scheduling results in more frequent use of varied teaching approaches and more student-centered environments. It helps teachers move away from discussion and lectures and into a more media-rich instruction. This flexibility allows more opportunities for cooperative teaching strategies such as **Team Teaching** and **Interdisciplinary Studies**. In addition, media-based instruction in block scheduling encourages student-centered activities and research projects. Such projects are coded in the Teacher's Wraparound Edition for *World History: The Human Experience*.

FOR FURTHER PROFESSIONAL READING...

Brett, M. 1996. Teaching Extended Class Periods. *Social Education* 60(2): 77–79.

Buckman, D.C., B.B. King, and S. Ryan. 1995. *Block Scheduling: Means to Improve School Climate.* Reston, Va.: National Association of Secondary Principals.

Caine, R.N., and G.C. Caine. 1993. *Teaching and the Human Brain: Making Connections.* Alexandria, Va.: Association of Supervision and Curriculum.

Carroll, J.M. 1994. "The Copernican Plan Evaluated: The Evolution of a Revolution." *Phi Delta Kappan* 76(2): 105–13.

Dorsch, N. 1994. "Making Connections: A Frames Analysis Perspective on the Implementation of an Innovative Pilot Program." Paper presented at the annual meeting of the Midwestern Educational Research Association, 12–15 October, at Chicago. ERIC ED 385 004.

Garner, H.G., ed. 1995. *Teamwork Models and Experience in Education.* Needham Heights, Mass.: Allyn and Bacon.

Gerking, J.L. 1995. "Building Block Schedules." *The Science Teacher* 62(4): 23–27.

Husband, R.E., and P.M. Short. 1994. *Middle School Interdisciplinary Teams: An Avenue to Greater Teacher Empowerment.* ERIC ED 372 043.

Kruse, C.A., and G.D. Kruse. 1995. "The Master Schedule and Learning: Improving the Quality of Education." NASSP *Bulletin* 79(571): 1–8.

National Education Commission of Time and Learning. 1994. *Prisoners of Time.* Washington, D.C.: U.S. Government Printing Office.

Nunan, D. 1988. *The Learner-Centered Curriculum.* Cambridge, England: Cambridge University Press.

Raker, R. 1994. *Integrated Block Scheduling and Team Teaching in the STEP-UP Academic English Program at Tokai International College.* ERIC ED 375 667.

Reid, L. 1995. *Perceived Effects of Block Scheduling on the Teaching of English.* Fort Collins, Colo.: Colorado State University. ERIC ED 382 950.

Shortt, T.L., and Y. Thayer. 1995. "What Can We Expect to See in the Next Generation of Block Scheduling?" *NASSP Bulletin* 79(571): 53–62.

Smith, S.C., and J.J. Scott. 1990. *The Collaborative School.* Eugene, Oregon: ERIC Clearinghouse on Educational Management; Reston, Va.: National Association of Secondary School Principals.

BLOCK SCHEDULING NOTES